Disclaimer

Although I do carry the title Doctor in front of my name, I do have to say I am not a licensed medical practitioner. However, I do have my PHD in Religious Studies. A master's degree in metaphysics.

Some of what I have degrees in may weave it's way into this books, but this is not about any one religion. This is a guide and nothing more . Use it as you see fit in order to build a better happier you.

This book in no way is a replacement for conventional therapy an should only be used as a tool and guide to finding a happier you.

Are You Happy: Everyday Happiness a Guide to Finding You

By:

Trient Press
3375 S Rainbow Blvd
#81710, SMB 13135
Las Vegas,NV 89180

Ordering Information:
Quantity sales. Special discounts are available on quantity purchases by corporations, associations, and others. For details, contact the publisher at the address above.
Orders by U.S. trade bookstores and wholesalers. Please contact Trient Press: Tel: (775) 996-3844; or visit www.trientpress.com.

Printed in the United States of America

Publisher's Cataloging-in-Publication data
Ruscsak, M.L.
A title of a book : Are You Happy: Everyday Happiness a Guide to Finding You

ISBN
 Paperback : 978-1-955198-19-6
  E-book :978-1-955198-20-2

Printed in the United States of America

ISBN
Paperback: 978-1-955198-19-6
eBook: 978-1-955198-20-2

Introduction

We all Hare it: Life would be that much easier if you loved yourself. Too many people live with low self-esteem…. Too many other people are simply indifferent toward themselves….

When was the last time your Mom or a friend asked if you were 'looking after yourself'? Can you honestly say that you are?

Too often, we place too much pressure on ourselves, or we expect too much of ourselves. We are constantly working hard toward our goals, and we beat ourselves up if we are anything other than perfect in that pursuit.

Is it any surprise we are often over-tired, malnourished, and depressed?

What a difference it would make if you spent time looking after yourself. If you surrounded yourself with friends who loved you, if you gave yourself a break every now and then, and if you told yourself you were doing great.

What if you really loved who you were, and you were satisfied with what you had?

Simply: you'd be content. You'd be healthier, happier, and more fulfilled. And that feeling would emanate from you and affect everyone you interacted with.

How do you get from here to there?

In this book, we will see that this requires a two-pronged assault. We need to change our thinking and the way we consider ourselves, and we also need to change the way we look after ourselves. What we eat, how we spend our time, and how we control our environment.

I liken this to looking after yourself the way a mother might look after her children. That means not only taking care of yourself physically by grooming, feeding, and making sure that everything else is done right – but also taking care of yourself emotionally.

When you're down, a good mother will tell you not to worry, and that you're great. If we treated ourselves like this and internalized that kind of affection, the world would be an easier, kinder place.

Each chapter in this book will tackle one of these aspects, and by the end we'll have a blueprint of self-care that will nourish our health, and our soul!

Chapter 1: Self-Care Using CBT and Mindfulness

Before we can talk about using CBT and mindfulness we first need to know what is it.

By definition:

Mindfulness-based cognitive therapy (MBCT) is a type of psychotherapy that combines cognitive therapy, meditation, and mindfulness.

Mindfulness-based cognitive therapy (MBCT) is an approach to psychotherapy that uses cognitive behavioral therapy (CBT) methods in collaboration with mindfulness meditative practices and similar psychological strategies. The origins to its conception and creation can be traced back to the traditional approaches from East Asian formative and functional medicine, philosophy and spirituality, birthed from the basic underlined tenants from classical Taoist, Buddhist and Traditional Chinese medical text, doctrine and teachings.

Ok, great now we know the text book meaning behind what we are about to learn. Please note this is not a over night fix. Changing how you think takes months and sometimes years. It requires putting in the work and sticking to it even when you want to quit. Using this book as a tool to help guide you but also using other tools that you have around you. And maybe changing the tools you are currently using.

But we will get to that later on. Right now we need to work in steps to help shape the YOU that YOU are wanting to be.

First, we need to start by changing the way we talk to ourselves. And this begins with mindfulness and CBT even if we don't call it that. However, in this guide we will.

Why am I stressing CBT?

CBT, or Cognitive Behavioural Therapy, is the current favourite approach in clinical psychology and it is going to be one of the most important tools in this book for transforming the way we view ourselves.

Remember when every counsellor you went to was using psychodynamic principles to treat patients, today they are all using CBT (or an integrative approach). While it's probably only a matter of time before a new school comes along and knocks CBT off the top spot, it still represents a powerful tool that the NHS in the UK and many others around the world have used to quickly and cheaply improve the lives of millions of patients. The 'quickly and cheaply' parts are also crucial as they mean that anyone can apply the principles and see immediate benefit, improving their self-esteem with no need to spend a ton of money and time on counselling.

Obviously if your symptoms persist you should seek professional help, but until then you can try some DIY to see if CBT is what you need to improve your self-concept. Again this a tool one of many we need to find our inner happiness.

A Brief History and Explanation

Essentially, CBT is composed of two concepts – behaviourism and cognitive psychology (as the name might suggest).

Behaviourism is the old school of thought that states how we learn to associate an event with an outcome to such a degree that we can begin treating the event as the outcome.

For example, in Pavlov's famous experiment using dogs, he taught his canine subjects to salivate at the sound of the bell by getting them used to hearing the bell while they ate.

This applies to your self esteem, in that you can end up having physical reactions to conditions where you're put under pressure. For example, you might find that in social situations you find yourself trembling or sweating as through your perception you've learned to associate them with leading to embarrassment or humiliation. Alternatively, you might find yourself feeling depressed or lethargic when you're attempting something new if you've failed several times in the past. Here the bad outcomes act as 'reinforcement', instructing you that your ambitions are doomed to failure. This is a learning mechanism that we've evolved which normally helps us to avoid making mistakes and which is generally adaptive in most situations. In modern society however there are times when it's misplaced and can be psychologically damaging.

Behavioural therapy to cure such associations involves 'reassociation'. This would mean teaching yourself to learn that putting yourself out on a limb can lead to positive outcomes too. You might achieve this by going to lots of social settings that you know you'll enjoy, or by trying lots of new things that you think you'll be good at.

Example; Think of a time that in you mind something negative happen when you put yourself out there. A new job, talking to a stranger. Anything. I bet you can think of that time without much thought at all.

Why?

In evolution we as a species had to learn that bad things cause negativing outcomes. Even death. Over time out thoughts have picked up on ques that has lead to the continued growth of our species. However, we as humans have taken it a different level. It not longer goes to basic survival it goes to us drawing back and being afraid to live .

Now, think of a time that you were afraid of putting yourself out there and it had a positive outcome. What changed between the two? Did you decide to just go for it? Or did the outcome just happen because you learned the skills that were needed for the desired outcome?

Neither is wrong but deciding the push past the fear is what CBT is all about. It is taking control of your thoughts and not letting the negative get in the way.

Another accept is actually looking at the friends you keep. As what they say goes to how our mindset is. Are the words they say to you positive or negative? Are they there to lift you up or hold you back from your version of happiness?

If you want a positive mindset you should also make sure you surround yourself with positive people who will compliment and encourage you rather than put you down. This way you will also be getting constant reinforcement that you're a worthwhile and capable person.

Since behaviourism though, psychology has moved on realizing that there is a conscious aspect in many of our problems. This is the crucial contribution that CBT makes by introducing a cognitive aspect to our brain and to our anxieties.

In the case of problems like low self-esteem, the cognitive aspect could be negative ruminations where you think about how everything will go wrong, negative self-talk or talking yourself out of doing things.

In the next chapter, we'll look at how you can use this important added component in order to silence the "inner critic" for greater peace and happiness.

Chapter 2: Silencing the Inner Critic

Out of all of the topics this may be the hardest. I can attest for me it was and still is. This is work that I have to do everyday for my own happiness and well-being.

The clinical part:

Patients with low self-esteem will often describe how they have a 'little voice' in the back of their head constantly telling them they're going to fail. Other concepts in CBT are 'over generalization', whereby you assume that because you've failed at one task you are going to fail at all tasks, and 'false hypotheses', where you incorrectly predict that you're going to fail at your tasks.

Now the hard work will begin. We will be employing CBT techniques in order to help you overcome this self-doubt.

Mindfulness

In the past few years CBT practitioners then have devised various methods that you can use to combat these problems. One of the most commonly used of these is actually borrowed from meditation and is known as 'mindfulness'. Here patients are instructed to find a quiet place and to sit down with their eyes closed. Much like in meditation they are then instructed to reflect on their inner thoughts.

This can be done while listening to calming music. Finding hertz meditation music online for the desired effect if you are also trying to manifest something into your reality.However, that is for advance meditation and will now help if you do not first focus on your overall mindset. There are several other ways to meditate which we will cover at another time. It is best to find the way that works best for you.

With meditation ,this doesn't mean that you should attempt to clear your mind however, merely 'watch' thoughts as they pass by without engaging in them, merely observing the content of your brains create passive thoughts as you might watch clouds passing in the sky. This way you can identify the kinds of things you are thinking and in particular any destructive thoughts you might be having.

As you get better at this you are should to be able to do it during day to day activities and then intervene; spotting the negative and damaging thoughts and seeing them for what they are. This will take practice and is not something that can be mastered overnight.

As you learn to master this you will begin to see that most negative ruminations are illogical and even if they aren't they certainly do more harm than good, so learning to spot them and then put an end to them is a valuable skill. Similarly, to aid in this culture of mindfulness, it helps if you keep a diary or journal of your thoughts and activities – then to read them back and see how anything you've said or done could be disruptive to you self- image.

Use the next few pages as a start to this mindfulness journal.

_____

_____

_____

_____

_____

_____

_____

_____

_____

_____

_____

_____

_____

_____

_____

_____

_____

_____

_____

_____

_____

_____

_____

_____

_____

_____

_____

_____

Positive Self-Talk

Another healthy practice to get into is Positive Self-Talk, or daily affirmations. Yes I know it sounds fufu, however, there is a great benefit to this.

You can also counter your negative thoughts with positive ones, utilizing 'positive self talk' to reaffirm your worth.As your words matter. What we tell ourselves matters more than what the outside world tell us.

Think about it for just a moment. When you look in the mirror do you say "I rock in this outfit" or do you say "I look horrible in this?" It could be the same outfit worn on different days, or maybe something new. Did someone we trust say we look good in the outfit or did someone we don't know say we looked bad? It all comes down to micro choices we make and what we tell ourselves.

Example : Personal story

When I was growing up I looked in the mirror every day. What I saw and told myself was that I was short, fat and ugly.A pimple faced geek with no friends.

How many of us can relate to this?

Now looking back at pictures from that same time. I was not fat, but I also was not extra thin. Short? Not really but I wasn't tall either when there were girls over 6 foot in my class.

Yet I let myself see the negative rather than telling myself , "I am cute." Lets start with a baby compliment .

Now , today I look in the mirror and give myself a pep talk before any activity that I'm doing. Why? Because when you tell yourself you CAN do something the negative fears slowly go away. Why? **Because your words matter**.

Activity:

Here you should make sure to focus on your good point, and to remember compliments you may have received in the past. Instead of telling yourself you're fat constantly, replace this with reminders about your nice eyes or straight teeth. You'd be surprised by how affective this can be.

Use the next few pages to write out your positive points.

_____

_____

_____

_____

_____

_____

_____

_____

Hypothesis Testing

Clinical Study:

Patients are also told to practice 'hypothesis testing', where they are encouraged to test their false hypotheses hopefully realizing that they are unfounded. For example, if a patient is scared to speak in public because they are concerned they'll stutter and fail, then they are encouraged to actually try speaking in public to find out if this is in fact the case. More often than not they'll find it isn't. This also works to prevent over generalization and again as a way to counter any negative associations they've developed.

So, if you're suffering from low self-esteem then you might want to try applying these principles to your life. Make sure you continue to go out and to challenge yourself, even if you genuinely are less than skilled at what it is you want to achieve this is the only way you are going to improve.

Becoming reclusive will only give you more time to ruminate and send you into a downward spiral. Similarly, surround yourself with positive friends and colleagues and try to focus on the good aspects of what you do. Support yourself with positive self-talk and try to catch yourself having negative thoughts and stamp them out. If this still doesn't work, then it's perhaps time to seek help from a professional who can talk you through the process.

Applying this to real life:

Everyday if we know it or not we continue to test our hypothesis on everything from getting up in front of a group of people to speak to approaching someone that we don't know.

Sometimes because of how we carry ourselves we self fulfil the hypothesis. We tell ourselves that we will fail before whatever we are trying even starts. Cause us to loose focus, momentum or even stuttering because we are afraid of failure.

Yet the same can be said when we tell ourselves "yes I can…" Just fill in the blank. When you tell yourself that yes you can do something your body language changes. This includes posture and being approachable.

So lets test the theory on paper so you can see it for yourself.

When was the last time you failed at something? What did you think would be the outcome before you attempted it?

_____

_____

_____

_____

_____

_____

_____
_____
_____
_____
_____
_____
_____
_____
_____
_____
_____
_____
_____
_____

When was the last time you said said I can do something even if you thought you would fail? What was the outcome?

_____
_____
_____
_____
_____
_____
_____
_____
_____
_____

_____
_____
_____
_____
_____
_____
_____
_____
_____
_____
_____
_____
_____
_____
_____
_____
_____
_____
_____
_____
_____
_____
_____
_____
_____
_____
_____
_____
_____

Chapter 3: Self-Fulfilling Prophecies

What is a self-fulfilling prophecy?

By definition:

A self-fulfilling prophecy describes a phenomenon by which what you believe to be true can actually become a reality by the fact that you actually believe it or that other people believe it.

If this sounds complicated then imagine an example. Say you're a boy at school who has an older brother who recently had the same teachers and proved very successful.

By this fact alone, the other teachers and pupils will assume that this new boy will achieve great grades too. This confidence and expectation will in turn rub off on him and he'll start to see himself as someone who has great academic ability.

(This is also a perfect example of how influences outside of our control can shape who we are – and why it is so important that we take matters back into our own hands!)

As you're probably aware, you tend to like things that you do well in and so by thinking you're good at academia you will then start to enjoy it more, and put in more time as a result. This is why sports psychologists use the 'sandwich' technique when giving criticism; that's positive, negative, positive.

The "Sandwich method" by definition:

The Compliment Sandwich (also called the Feedback Sandwich or Criticism Sandwich), beyond being one of the worst management techniques ever invented, was created as a way of trying to give somebody constructive criticism without making them feel bad.

This way they can get across their advice without damaging the esteem of the sprinter or gymnast. Science has proven using this method the athlete will constantly increase their own self-esteem and closely control how they perceive themself in order to increase their own success.

Putting this into action:

In the same way that we tell ourselves that we are bad at something and then try it to see that we are "bad" at it. We need to say we are good at it or I need more practice.

In the way that an athlete constantly works to better their skill we need to work on task to be better at them.

For example : You put in for a promotion at work and didn't get it. Did you first see if you have the skills that were needed? You probably did , or you were willing to learn the skills.

However, when we think back to mindset it's not always as cut and dry as a promotion at work. We tend to lean to smaller things. Do I look good for this date? Is this my color? It can be anything really.

It all depends on what you tell yourself. If you decide the negative is true . Then the outcome is already destined to be negative. However, if you tell yourself the positive then you have a greater chance at a positive outcome. As Long as the desired outcome is within a reasonable limit.

The Law of Attraction

What is the law of attraction?

By definition:

The law of attraction is the attractive, magnetic power of the Universe that manifests through everyone and through everything.

It is part of the creative power of the Universe. Even the law of gravity is part of the law of attraction.

This law attracts thoughts, ideas, people, situations, circumstances, and the things you think about.

The law of attraction manifests through your mind, thoughts and imagination, and is the tool for creating your reality, as you want it.

It draws to you thoughts and ideas of a similar kind, people who think like you, and situations and circumstances that you repeatedly think about.

So what does that mean?

How you perceive yourself also speaks volumes to other people.It will reveal your self confidence in subtle ways – the way you walk, the way you speak and the way you dress and the way you act.

If you act as though you deserve respect then you'll start to believe it yourself and if you start to believe it then so will others.

This actually goes deeper than abstract opinions as it can even be used to generate wealth and success.

For example, by dressing well and wearing nice watches (knock-offs will do, no one will know) you eventually be able to afford them. If you project an image of being wealthy then others will begin to think you're rich and successful. This can mean that your boss is more likely to give you a promotion (**this is why they say you should dress for the job you want, not the job you're in**). It also means others will be more likely to trust you in business and that other wealthy people will gravitate towards you (**like attracts like**).

Even the gifts you receive will be more expensive on average as you generally tend to spend more on gifts for people who own more expensive things – otherwise it won't fit with the décor and you'll look cheap. If you act confident with the opposite sex then they'll assume you're in high demand and as such will find you more attractive. It

His is why dressing well can make others believe you are successful and can make you feel successful too.

Personal story:

Shortly after my daughter was born I started working at a local restaurant. Now mind you my self esteem was extremely low. My mind set was this job is the best I could do. Minimum wage, no benefits…. so on and so forth. However, the co-owner ; I'll call her Linda , took me aside as she saw potential in me. Over time when I was off work I found myself dressing better, feeling more confident about myself which showed in the my work performance, customer service and all aspects of the job. Leading to being promoted to GM .

It wasn't just changing the clothing I wore it was acting the part. It's part of things those around have been saying for years yet I had tuned out.

Advice
Putting on your best clothes helps to make you feel good while wearing them – The second part is don't just look the part though – act the part, and over time by mimicking the

actions and behaviour of someone successful you'll start to pick them up as habits. Wish you spoke more clearly and slowly? They forcibly put that voice and manner on and over time you will develop it as your normal behaviour.

Activity

Go to your closet and actually look at what you have. It brand names don't matter, but really look at the styles of clothing.

Make areas in your closet.
What is you around the house things?
What makes you feel successful. Those are your power clothes.
What do you wear to work? Is there a way to upgrade your work cloths to better show where you want to be in terms of success?

Chapter 4: Looking After Looks

One of the biggest reasons many people suffer from low confidence is that they're unhappy with a physical feature – or indeed all of their physical features. If this describes you, then you should be pleased to know that there is a lot you can do about your physical features, and there's a fair chance you're not maximizing your potential. Here's how to play the hand you're dealt and get yourself looking like a million dollars.

Advice

It's in the Little Things – How to Feel Taller

Firstly, appearance needn't necessarily mean your face, and for many men in particular low confidence can stem from not being as tall as they'd like to be. Even if this isn't a particular source of contention for you, adding a bit of extra height will automatically help you to feel more confident as you look down on people, or at least look at them at eye level, rather than constantly looking up.

But it's impossible to make yourself grow taller right? Well yes and no. Basically, rather than actually growing taller yourself, you can make yourself appear taller by investing in insoles that increase your height. If you type into e-bay 'tall insoles' you'll find several products along the lines of what you're looking for. These only cost a small amount and can be easily slipped inside your shoe then adjusted to be taller or shorter up to around four inches.

Four inches of extra height if the shoes you're wearing allow it, take you from a short-ish five nine to a fairly tall six foot one. If you combine this with fairly large shoes you can be really rather tall. For women the same can be true of high heels, and as an added bonus these also make women stand up taller and improve their gait and stride – you can't shuffle in heels.

For men bulking up will also make you more imposing and as you generally fill up more space you'll feel more commanding and confident (more on this in an upcoming chapter). Try eating large amounts of protein along with regular exercise and work in particular on your chest and shoulders to create an imposing silhouette.

It's hard to feel insecure when you're over six foot and covered in muscle. At the same time men who are conscious about their weight should make sure to do a lot of CV and avoid fatty foods to get themselves feeling leaner and less chubby – perhaps you need to take up less space.

Likewise, for women, toning your abs and tightening your behind can make you feel sexier and again improve your silhouette. To help you along the way you can always use underwear that holds in the fatter areas and plumps out the bits that need plumping.

Girdles and corsets are the best known but you can also get pants that support your bottom. Girdles also exist for guys and while it may be a bit embarrassing, they can at the same time make you feel more confident when you're out and about – no one need know!

How to Beam

You know what also makes a huge difference to the way you feel though? Posture.

In the last section, we saw the power of feeling taller or bigger. This can make you physically take up more space, which in turn can drastically increase confidence.

But simply by pulling your shoulders back and holding your chin up, you can have a very similar effect. Not only that, but this has a physiological impact on your mood, which helps you to feel more positive and confidant.

Activity

Two great places to learn self confidence is either by taking acting/ modeling classes or martial arts classes.

For modeling classes it does not matter if you are 16 or 60. This is not about being the next big thing this is about learning how to walk, talk and be comfortable in your own skin. Who knows it may lead to being found.

For martial arts, please consult a doctor before getting to this. Although for both physical posture and gaining a lot in self confidence and discipline , you also want to be in the right kind of martial arts class.

Make a list.

What classes are open right now? What do you hope to gain from them? How much time does each class take per day? Per week? How much does the classes cost?

_____

_____

_____

_____

_____

_____

_____

_____

_____

_____

_____

_____

_____

_____
_____
_____
_____
_____
_____
_____
_____
_____
_____
_____
_____
_____

Advice

Putting Your Best Face On

Inserting additional lifts into your shoes might all be a bit extreme though, and if it's just your facial features you're concerned about there's still a lot you can achieve without resorting to surgery.

Firstly, make sure you get a haircut somewhere nice and one that fits the shape of your face.

The squarer your jaw the more rounded a cut you'll need and vice versa as a general rule. If you're male you also need to think about facial hair, and while this is generally a fashion mistake it can sometimes really improve your looks – just look at Rowan Atkinson in Mr Bean compared to the same guy in Blackadder.

Another trick to try you might also want to try dying your hair to see if another color suits you better. There is no rule that says the color you're born with is the color you need to keep. It's ok to experiment. Temporary colors work great for this, then work up to the more permanent.

If you're a woman you have the benefit of being able to enhance your features with make-up. This means using foundation to cover up spots and blemishes and blusher to bring a bit more colour to your cheeks. Often those who are a little shy will try to dress and apply makeup minimally so as not to draw attention to themselves. However, this attempt to 'hide' in plain sight can cause all the same self-fulfilling prophecy effects that we have previously looked at. In other words, you shrink away, and people assume that you don't want to be seen.

If you get professional advice on how to do your makeup you can maximize your good features and up your sex appeal even if you can't aid your natural beauty. A professional from somewhere like 'Color Me Beautiful' will tell you not only which colors suit you best, but also what your best features are.

Normally, you will be told to focus on either your eyes or your lips, depending on which is your stronger feature, and then apply the heaviest amount of makeup here to draw the eyes to your assets and away from your flaws.

So if you have nice lips you might be advised to use some bright red lipstick to make them look fuller and more inviting, while if you're strongest feature is your eyes you might be recommended to use a heavy eye shadow or eye liner to make them stand out. Generally, it's best not to go to heavy on both as you can end up looking like a porn star or as though you're just trying too hard, and while your colors should be bold they shouldn't look as though you're wearing face paint – natural looking colors that suit your skin tone are to be advise.

Prefer a more natural look? That's fine too – but that doesn't mean not using any makeup at all. It just means being more subtle, and carefully highlighting your best features.

This will take practice and will not happen over night. And member it's only make-up it comes off with a little water.

Advice
Grooming

Both men and women should also make sure they groom properly. For women that means removing any stray facial hairs and moisturizing regularly. For men, that again means moisturizing to be rid of dead skin as well as trimming their nasal hairs and ear hairs which can be very foul if neglected. At the same time use whitening toothpastes and maybe even specific whitener to give your teeth a glow.

Alternatively, a nicer set of glasses or a cool pair of sunglasses can improve your face and make you look intelligent or cool depending on your desired look. Spend a little more on the things that you use to decorate and adorn your face.

Basically the take home message is not to give up on your looks. As long as you put effort into your appearance and ask friends for honest advice, you'll look better and feel better about yourself. There's nothing wrong with cutting a few corners or using a few sneaky tricks to improve the way you look and if you look good, you'll feel good.

It's not even just about the way you look thanks to your grooming – it's also about the way it feels. Taking the time to look after yourself is a physical reminder that you do care about your looks (**and yourself by extension**). This is a chance to unwind, and the feeling of running a razor over your skin and opening up those pores can be extremely cathartic – like you're letting go of the day's stresses.

Why not spend a little more on a high-tech bathroom and invest in a walk-in shower, or even a hot tub? You could get yourself a steam room and turn your home into a mini spa.

Spa breaks themselves also come highly recommended for both men and women. Having someone attentive to your needs, being pampered, and coming away smelling and looking great… these all make a huge difference to the way you look, feel, and present yourself!

Chapter 5: Taking Care of Your Health

One sure fire way to improve your self-esteem is by exercising. The obvious reason for this is that you'll improve your physique which will make you more attractive and more capable. You won't feel as physically threatened by other people, you'll win respect from others who are impressed by your new shape or envious even (you'll find that you become a font of knowledge for anyone who wants to do the same), you'll be better at sports and all physical activities, and you'll be more attractive to the opposite sex.

Not bad right?

The Basic 8 exercises

1. Squat

One of the purest tests of strength, the squat incorporates almost all of the muscles in your legs and core, says Yellin. The GIF above shows a bodyweight squat, which is a good way to nail down your form. Once your form is solid, you can add weight by holding dumbbells or a bar in front of your shoulders (front squat), resting a barbell on your back (back squat), or holding a weight in front of you at your chest (goblet squat).

● Stand with your feet slightly wider than hip-width apart.

- Lower your hips into a squat as you bend your knees and keep your back flat.
- Continue to lower yourself until your thighs are parallel to the floor.
- Push into the floor through your heels to return to start. That's 1 rep.
- Keep your heels flat and knees aligned with your second toe so they don't cave in.

The squat targets your glutes, quads, and core muscles. If this is too difficult, try starting with a chair squat: Squat in front of a chair (or bench) and lightly tap your butt to the chair with each rep.

2. Deadlift

Deadlifts are considered hands-down one of the best exercises to train the backside of your body, namely your glutes and hamstrings. And because you're working from a stable base, you can really load up the weight on these. There are a bunch of different varieties of deadlifts, like the Romanian (as pictured above, where you lower the weight as you hip hinge), traditional barbell (where you pull the weight from the floor), and sumo (with a wider stance and toes pointing out at about a 45-degree angle.)

Proper form is essential to protect your lower back, so it's a good idea to practice with a lighter weight in front of a mirror until you feel comfortable with the exercise. Remember to lift with your legs, not with your back. (That's important for pretty much every exercise, by the way, but especially with the deadlift.) If you don't have a barbell, you can use a pair of heavy dumbbells or even a loop resistance band.

- Stand with your feet hip-width apart, knees slightly bent, and arms relaxed by the front of your quads, with a dumbbell in each hand. This is the starting position.
- Hinge forward at your hips and bend your knees slightly as you push your butt way back. Keeping your back flat, slowly lower the weight along your shins. Your torso should be almost parallel to the floor.
- Keeping your core engaged, push through your heels to stand up straight and return to the starting position. Keep the weight close to your shins as you pull up.
- Pause at the top and squeeze your butt. That's 1 rep.

The deadlift is a hip-hinging movement that targets the hamstrings and glutes. It also engages your shoulders, back, and core.

3. Glute Bridge

Glute bridges (also called hip bridges) target one of the largest muscles in the lower body—the glutes, says Yellin. They also contribute to building leg strength and core stabilization.

- Lie on your back with your knees bent and feet flat on the floor, hip-width apart. Hold a dumbbell in each hand and rest the weights right under your hip bones. This is the starting position.
- Squeeze your glutes and abs, and push through your heels to lift your hips a few inches off the floor, until your

body forms a straight line from your shoulders to your knees.

- Hold for a second and then slowly lower your hips to return to the starting position. This is 1 rep.

The glute bridge is a hip-extension exercise that primarily targets the glutes, but it also engages the hamstrings and the core muscles. If you've never done a glute bridge before, ditch the weights and do it with just your body-weight first—it's still an effective move without added resistance.

4. Push-Up

Being able to move your own body weight is one of the best signs of strength, says Fagan. If a regular push-up from the floor is too challenging at first, you can modify it by elevating your hands on a step or a table—the higher your hands, the easier it will be.

- Start in a high plank with your palms flat on the floor, hands shoulder-width apart, shoulders stacked directly above your wrists, legs extended behind you, and core and glutes engaged.
- Bend your elbows and lower your body to the floor. Drop to your knees if needed.
- Push through the palms of your hands to straighten your arms. That's 1 rep.

The push-up is a push or press movement that works all the pressing muscles in the upper body, including your chest, shoulders, and triceps. It can help you improve your strength and form when performing dumbbell or barbell chest presses.

5. Bent-Over Row

Working on increasing your rowing strength can also help you complete your first body-weight pull-up—a challenging exercise that's also an excellent indicator of strength, says Fagan. (A resistance band can assist you with a pull-up.)

- Stand with your feet hip-width apart, holding a dumbbell in each hand with your arms at your sides.
- With your core engaged, hinge forward at the hips, pushing your butt back. Bend your knees and make sure you don't round your shoulders. (Your hip mobility and hamstring flexibility will dictate how far you can bend over.)
- Gaze at the ground a few inches in front of your feet to keep your neck in a comfortable, neutral position.
- Perform a row by pulling the weights up toward your chest, keeping your elbows close to your body, and squeezing your shoulder blades for 2 seconds at the top of the movement. Your elbows should go past your back as you bring the weight toward your chest.
- Slowly lower the weights by extending your arms toward the floor. That's 1 rep.

This bent-over row is a pulling exercise that uses all of the pulling muscles in your upper body, including the back, shoulders, and biceps, says Yellin. "It also requires leg and core engagement to maintain a strong position," he adds.

6. Hollow-Body Hold

"The hollow-body hold is such an amazing total-body exercise for maintaining core stability," says Fagan. This core strength translates to a stronger foundation for many of your other compound moves, like the pull-up and deadlift, she adds.

- Lie faceup on a mat with your legs extended and arms straight over your head, keeping them close to your ears.
- Contract your abs to press your lower back into the ground.
- Point your toes, squeeze your thighs together, squeeze your glutes, and lift your legs off the ground.
- Lift your shoulders off the ground and keep your head in a neutral position so that you're not straining your neck. Your legs and mid-back should both be off the floor, and you should be in the shape of a banana, with just your lower back and hips on the ground.
- Hold this position for as long as you can while maintaining proper form.

The hollow-body hold is an isometric exercise that targets all the muscles in your core. If the traditional hollow-body hold is too difficult, you can modify it by bending your knees or keeping your arms forward instead of overhead.

7. Dumbbell Chopper

It's important to get comfortable with rotational movements that have you twisting your spine in a safe way. The wood-chop exercise is a great one to start with—stick with just your body weight until you get the hang of it. You can hold a hand towel or another small object in your hands to help keep your arms straight.

This will help give you a sense of what rotating your torso should feel like, and it may even be a feel-good stretch after sitting all day.

- Stand with your feet wider than hip-width apart, core engaged, hands clasped together or holding a small towel (or dumbbell once you've progressed) in both hands by your left leg.
- Raise your arms diagonally in front of your body to the upper right of your reach, allowing your torso and toes to naturally rotate to the right as you twist.
- Now "chop" the weight down to the left, bringing it across the front of your body and aiming for your left ankle, allowing your torso and toes to naturally rotate in that direction. Focus on keeping your lower body stable and rotating from your core. This is 1 rep.
- Do all your reps on one side, and then switch sides and repeat.

The woodchopper exercise targets the muscles of the core, specifically the obliques. It also works the legs and glutes. An added bonus: It will give your heart rate a little boost.

8. Reverse Lunge

Or, insert any other single-leg exercise here. Whether we're talking about a single-leg deadlift, a step-up, or a reverse lunge (as pictured), single-leg or "unilateral" exercises are vital in helping you get stronger since they can correct strength imbalances, says Fagan. And that helps you get stronger in your bilateral moves (those that work both sides of your body at the same time).

Added bonus: Single-leg moves also require a ton of core stability, so you're getting in some ab work, too. Try them without additional weight until you get your balance down.

- Stand with your feet about shoulder-width apart and engage your core.
- Step backward with your right foot, landing on the ball of your right foot and keeping your right heel off the ground.
- Bend both knees to 90 degrees as you sink into a lunge. Focus on keeping your core engaged and your hips tucked (don't stick your butt out). Sometimes it can be helpful to place your hands on your hips so you can make sure your hips aren't tilting to the side or forward and back.
- Push through the heel of your left foot to return to your starting position. You can do all of your reps in a row, or you can alternate sides.

The reverse lunge is a single-leg exercise that works the glutes, legs, and core. Most people find it to be easier on the knees than a forward lunge. It's also slightly easier in terms of balance and stability since you have better control of momentum when you're pushing off from the back foot to return to standing.

That's not all exercise is about however. If you train regularly you'll soon find that it affects you in ways that you wouldn't have expected. Training your body is something you can do regularly that has a visible and practical effect. Over time you will see that you're directly controlling an aspect of yourself. Every time you go to the gym you come away a little bit better than you were before you go in and that's one productive thing you've done that day.

Even more, when you're in the gym, trying to run an extra mile on the treadmill or lift an extra 10kg on the bench press, you're testing yourself and coming out better.

You're challenging yourself and overcoming it on a daily basis – over time you'll learn that you can do the same in any aspect of your life. Working out is a truly life affirming activity that can help you to grow both mentally and literally physically.

Working out will also increase your mood, and so your self- esteem, in other ways too. The actual act of working out causes your body to release the feel-good hormone serotonin. On top of that it also leads to neurogenesis, the birth of new brain cells. In short training will lift your mood and improve your cognitive performance both immediately and over time.

Getting Started With a Fitness Regime

To begin training then you need to assess your current condition. If you're currently overweight you need to be doing large amounts of CV (that's aerobic exercise such as running or sprinting) and cutting your caloric intake. If you're currently very thin you need to do the opposite – using fewer repetitions of a heavier weight while increasing the amount of protein you eat (that's meats and dairy products).

You can even take either a protein shake or a weight gainer to supplement your diet. Similarly, to lose weight you need to train more regularly – about five times a week, but to get stronger and larger you need to train more heavily and less often to give your muscles time to recover and build.

To begin with you can train using a simple full body routine. While 'split' routines and the like are more conducive to training when you're more advanced, to start with you need to get your body used to training.

Each session should last about forty minutes, and each exercise should consist of three sets – that means you lift the weight however many times, take a rest then repeat for three sets. Once you begin to see progress start reading into the process in more detail and learn the tricks and techniques used by the pros.

The most important thing though is that you find a program and then stick with it. Even if that program isn't perfect, it will bring some results simply due to the fact that you're doing some kind of training. That also means it's much better to do something very simple two or three times a week, rather than being too ambitious right away. Adherence is what really matters here.

Sample Workout log

Exercise	Saturday	Sunday	Monday	Tuesday	Wednesday	Thursday	Friday
	#/Time	#/Time	#/Time	#/Time	#/Time	#/Time	#/Time
Squat							
Deadlift							
Glute Bridge							
Push-Up							
Bent-Over Row							
Dumbbell Chopper							
Reverse Lunge							

Nourishing Nutrition and Sleep

Nutrition can make a huge difference to the way you feel about yourself and to your mood in general. That's partly because your diet will impact on your looks and your energy levels, but also because it can directly influence your mood.

Foods that contain vitamin C for example will improve your mood because they provide an influx of serotonin –

vitamin C being used to make serotonin. Likewise, foods high in tryptophan will do the same thing.

Almost any food will trigger a release of dopamine, which is a reward hormone. Conversely, if you don't eat regularly, you will have high cortisol leading to stress and anxiety.

Foods high in zinc, magnesium, and vitamin D (among others) can all help to increase testosterone production, which in men and women is closely linked with enhanced mood, energy, and drive.

Conversely though, foods that are high in processed sugars can cause low level inflammation. This is modulated through the release of pro-inflammatory cytokines, which can also affect the brain. Ever wondered why you feel sad and low energy when you have a cold or stomach bug? Brain inflammation is quite possibly the answer!

Simple sugars and processed foods (especially acellular carbs) can also negatively impact the 'gut microbiome'. This means that they can feed the bad bacteria that live in our guts and starve the good ones. That in turn has a big impact on mood and energy, seeing as these bacteria release numerous neurotransmitters and hormones, and play a big role in energy metabolism.

Sugary foods also spike the blood with sugar and insulin, which then quickly dissipates. This results in a 'crash' where blood sugar is low and cortisol is high again.

Of course, processed, simple sugars also typically don't contain healthy nutrients (hence the term 'empty calories') which means you don't get all the hormone and mood support you get from the good stuff.

So if you want to feel good, then you need to eat well. Treat yourself yes, but do so by using fruits, vegetables, yogurts, and other healthy treats. That way, you'll feel better in the short term AND the long term.

Recipes

Fruity Maple Glazed Ham Recipe
A yummy recipe from Ocean Spray
Ingredients:

1 8-ounce can Ocean Spray® Jellied Cranberry Sauce
1/4 cup maple syrup
1 8-pound fully-cooked whole boneless ham

Instructions:

Combine cranberry sauce and maple syrup in a small saucepan.
Cook over medium heat just until sauce is smooth, whisking frequently.
Place ham on rack in a shallow roasting pan.

Insert meat thermometer in thickest part of ham.

Bake, uncovered, in a 325° oven for 1 1/2 to 2 hours or until thermometer registers 135° to 140 °.

Liberally baste ham with glaze during the last 45 minutes of baking.

Makes 24 servings.

New England Cornbread Stuffing
A yummy recipe from Ocean Spray

Ingredients:

2 cups cornbread stuffing
1/2 pound sausage meat, cooked, drained and crumbled
3/4 cup Craisins® Sweetened Dried Cranberries
1/3 cup chopped pecans
1 teaspoon thyme
1/2 cup chicken broth

Instructions:

Preheat oven to 350°.

Combine all ingredients, except chicken broth, in a medium casserole dish.

Add chicken broth; mix well.

Add more chicken broth for a moister stuffing.

Cover and bake for 30 minutes or until heated through.

Makes about 3 cups.

.

Sleep

Sleep is just as important. Sleeping poorly will cause your physical appearance to deteriorate, as well as your mental health and your mood. Bad sleep causes bags under the eyes, bloodshot eyes, blotchy-red skin, and the deterioration of hair and nails over time. It also leads to weight gain.

In the short term, poor sleep will leave you with low energy, and will increase stress hormones like adrenaline and cortisol. You'll be wired, anxious, and fraught.

The solution is to sleep longer, and to sleep better! Consider this a crucial aspect of your self-care, that will help you to look and feel your very best.

Here are some key tips to consider:

Get at least 8 hours every night - this is non-negotiable!

Aim to go to bed at the same time each night. Our bodies love predictability.

Find out your own 'chronotype' by experimenting. What times work best for you to sleep and wake up?

Take a hot shower or bath before bed

No technology 1 hour before sleep. Read a book and try to stay calm. This is 'winding down' time.

We can also use a little CBT to fall asleep faster. Instead of worrying about not getting enough sleep or trying to force yourself to sleep, instead focus on just enjoying the relaxation. The irony is that when you do this, you fall asleep much faster!

Write your answers here	
Time I go to sleep:	
Time I get up:	
Number of hours of sleep at night:	
My sleep distractions include:	
My transition to sleep ● An hour before I go to bed I . .	
● A half hour before I go to bed I . . .	
● Right before I go to bed I. . .	
What I need to change in order to get enough sleep	

What I can change in my life in order to get enough sleep:	
What I cannot change:	

Sample Worksheets

Activity

Keep a Sleep Diary

Fill in data and observations about your sleep for five nights in a row (make sure to include one weekend night). Then, design a research question and hypothesis to test in Week 2.

🕐 Sleep Diary	DAY 1 /	DAY 2 /	DAY 3 /	DAY 4 /	DAY 5 /
EVENING · I consumed caffeine today. (Examples: soda, chocolate, tea, coffee, sports/energy drink)					
Morning					
Afternoon					
Evening					
I exercised for 20 or more minutes.					
Morning					
Afternoon					
Evening					
I took a nap today. Y/N					
I felt tired today. Y/N					
Morning					
Afternoon					
Evening					
NIGHT · My mood today: (G) good (O) OK (B) bad					
Activities I did 1–2 hours before bed: (Examples: took a shower, messaged with friends, watched a video, finished homework, read a book, etc.)					
I went to bed at:	AM PM	AM PM	AM PM	AM PM	AM PM
I woke up this morning at:	AM PM	AM PM	AM PM	AM PM	AM PM
I got out of bed this morning at:	AM PM	AM PM	AM PM	AM PM	AM PM
MORNING · Falling asleep last night was: (E) easy; (O) OK; (D) difficult					
I woke up during the night. Y/N					
I slept for a total of _____ hours.					
I woke up feeling: (R) refreshed; (T) a little tired; (VT) very tired					

Organize Your Argument

Ready to use your sleep-diary data and research to craft a persuasive argument? Choose a prompt below. Then organize your position, claims, and evidence with this planner.

A. How should schools use the science of circadian rhythms to improve students' lives?

B. How will YOU apply the science of circadian rhythms to improve your life?

> You might want to consider ideas like school start times; breaks for exercise, nutrition, stress relief, or rest; strategies and supports for flagging energy; homework expectations; scheduling of extra-curricular activities; and blue light from electronic devices.

Persuasive Argument Planner

Introduction
- ▶ Hook/get reader's attention (e.g., introduce a stat or a question)
- ▶ Explain your chosen topic
- ▶ State your position

	Claim 1	Claim 2	Claim 3
Claims Craft two or more claims to support your position (your argument). For example: Schools should _____ because that would help students who _____ to _____.			
Supporting Evidence Provide research, facts, and scientific findings to support each claim.			

Conclusion
- ▶ Restate your position
- ▶ Summarize your argument and supporting evidence
- ▶ Write a concluding statement and call to action

Chapter 6: Letting Go of Regrets

Regretting the past is something that we all know we shouldn't do
– and that we all know is pointless – and yet we all still also have a tendency to do it.

Unfortunately, regretting mistakes is something that is largely out of our control. We are programmed you see to learn from mistakes because in the wild it would have helped us to avoid making similar mistakes in future. We regret touching fire pretty much as soon as we try it, and thus we are very unlikely to the same thing twice.

But in our evolutionary history our mistakes had a tendency to be much more clear cut and avoidable in future. T mistakes we make today tend to be more complicated and dwelling on them tends to be less useful.

Let's take that guy or girl you liked ten years ago for instance. They were giving clear hints of interest and wanted you to make a move, but you were too shy. You've moved on since then and you're happily in a new relationship, but it doesn't stop you from regretting that past mistake. Which is really just a bit infuriating.

Likewise, you might have made a mistake in your career once. Maybe you lost an important document which lost the company thousands, and that led to you being demoted. Or maybe you made a mistake when you shouted at your friend in haste. These are mistakes you can't 'undo' and that you knew were wrong at the time – no future victory is going to erase them and they'll keep playing over and over again in your head until you go mad.

Or will they?

Do Regrets Fade With Time?

If you're reading this chapter, it's probably because you're struggling with some regret whether it was a small recent mistake or a big screw up, then you're probably hoping that I'm going to tell you it goes away. I wish I could, but unfortunately I regret to say that the evidence isn't quite so clear cut.

According to one study by Gilovich et al., published in Psychological Review, some regrets will heal over time, but others will be less likely to.

That's because there are two types of regret: regrets of commission and regrets of omission. Regrets of commission are regrets about things you did, while regrets of omission are regrets about things you did not do.

Guess which ones we regret for the longest time?

That's right – we regret the things we don't do for longer and in fact those regrets tend never to heal (though I can think of at least one example in my personal history that largely goes against that).

This seems like a clear message to 'grab life by the horns' as it were and to 'do more stuff', but again it's probably a little more complicated than that…

That Which Has Been Done…

The first thing I noticed when thinking about this study was that chances you didn't take tend to be easier to rectify than those you did. 'That which has been done, cannot be undone', and yet 'that which is not done may yet be done'. In other words, if you're regretting not doing something still… then an obvious solution is to simply do it now. Pick up the phone and get talking to the one that got away!

The other point to consider is that the whole concept of 'paths not taken' is one that is somewhat arbitrary at best. The reason we regret the things we don't do most is no doubt because we never find out. We have an idealised version of how those things would have turned out in our heads so we regret not living that possible reality. Meanwhile the things we did do we got to see in the cold light of day – thus they tend to be considerably less interesting.

Let's say you always wanted to move to Australia as a child. You choose not to because you are afraid, you don't have the money, you think it's unwise etc. and thus you spend the rest of your years wondering what it would have been like and regretting your decision not to.

You may have done many other miraculous things your life – whether that's getting married and having children, being there to support your family or winning the Nobel Peace Prize… the problem is that you know what that was like and it was imperfect. Thus the 'undone' things always seem more interesting. Likewise the mistakes you make you live through and so you decide they could never have been that bad.

And what you also must realise is that it's actually completely required that you do turn down some of what life has to offer. Very often in order to experience one thing we must necessarily turn down something else. There are billions of options open to you every single second and yet you will always just choose one of them. That's an infinite undone-to-done ratio.

This might sound depressing – as though you'll never be happy with what you decide – and it's very much a case of 'the grass is always greener'. But in reality what I'm saying is that the grass always seems greener on the other side. It's not, and what you've done is probably perfectly remarkable and worthwhile in its own right: you just have to learn to see that.

But Will it Pass?

If you can reframe the way you look at your roads 'untaken' then, you might find that you can overcome that feeling of regret. But would they fade over time as time went on even if you never managed this, or does the study prove that they will never go away?

To be honest, the research seems to suggest that our regrets won't completely fade – and particularly when they're related to things we didn't do.

But I heard a nice way of looking at this recently when watching VSauce on YouTube. In an episode titled 'Mistkaes' (get it?) the presenter Michael paraphrases a friend of his. That friend told him that past mistakes were like carvings in a tree. They don't grow with the tree – they don't even get higher. Nor do they tend to fade and in fact in some cases they can get darker.

However, while the marks don't change, the tree does and over time it grows to become significantly huger leaving the marks as a relative 'dot' in the bark. In other words, the carving that once took up a big proportion of the tree is now just a tiny mark on a huge tree – just a very small part of that tree's history.

Your mistakes are similar. They might not go away, but as you build on them and have more experiences you will find that you can bury them. They're a part of who you are and actually you shouldn't want that any other way – however they are an increasingly insignificant part of who you are. The key is to accept them and grow anyway.

Activity

Journal Exercise

Write down the decision or situation you deeply regret.

_____

_____

_____

_____

_____

_____

_____

_____

_____

_____

_____

_____

_____

_____

_____

_____

_____

_____

_____

_____

_____

_____

_____

_____

_____

Reflect on why you regret it. What about it do you regret? Did certain negative consequences cause problems in your life?

_____

_____

_____

_____

_____

_____

_____

_____

_____

_____

_____

_____

_____

_____

_____

_____

_____

_____

_____

_____

_____

_____

_____

_____

_____

_____

Reflect on whether you'd do anything differently if you were in the same situation in the future. Write down your response.

_____

_____

_____

_____

_____

_____

_____

_____

_____

_____

_____

_____

_____

_____

Chapter 7: The Power of Gratitude and Self Compassion

There is a specific type of regret that is particularly hard to let go of: the kind where you blame yourself.

Thus, one more powerful tip for being happier, calmer, and more fulfilled? Occasionally just cut yourself some slack. Most of us are extremely harsh on ourselves: more so than we ever would be with anyone else. We expect too much, and we don't allow for simple mistakes or slips. In short: we demand perfection and we rarely give ourselves a break.

When was the last time you said something you wished you hadn't, or you didn't finish as much work as you wanted to?

And how did you spend the rest of that day? Most likely, you spent it regretting your shortcomings and feeling stressed.

Perhaps you let it eat at your self-esteem, or you felt you didn't deserve nice things.

Even if it was just cheating on your diet, you may have beaten yourself up something rotten!

Now ask yourself: how would you have reacted had someone else told you those same things? You'd no doubt have given them a break and been kind to them. So how about you be the same with yourself?

This is another example of mindfulness – of being mindful of the kinds of things you are thinking, and how those things affect your mind and your mood. Are your thoughts healthy? Or are they actually quite damaging?

One way to change your thoughts from a CBT perspective, is to try using mantras. Combine this with post-it-notes around your home that contain those notes in order to improve your mood and remind yourself to think more positively.

For this to work well, those notes should be things that you already believe are true to some extent. So if you feel that you are intelligent, then write a note reminding yourself of that.

And if you feel that you have an attractive ass… write that down too and stick it in your bathroom!

One more very important reminder that you should write in capital letters and place where you will see it the first moment you wake up?

BE KIND TO YOURSELF

Journaling can help to. Write down three things you did well today, and any compliments that people gave you. You can then read these back from time to time! This has a huge impact, seeing as for most of us, an insult has a much bigger impact on our self- image than a compliment. This practice forces you to skew that balance.

Loving Kindness Meditation and Gratitude

You can also practice being kinder to yourself with something called 'loving kindness meditation'. This is a form of meditation that involves spending time cultivating a feeling of kindness toward yourself. Bask in that feeling, and let it really sink in. Focus on this sensation and try to maintain it for 10 minutes at a time, a few times a week. It's truly transformative in the way you see the world.

Finally, consider cultivating a gratitude attitude. This means focusing on the things you have, and the things you are happy with. This not only makes you more positive, but it brings you into the present moment and helps you to feel better about the things that you have accomplished already. It's a perfect way to combat those feelings of regret!

In that journal, you should also write down 3 things that you are grateful for at the end of every day. This will force you to reflect on how much has gone right and how much is good in your life.

Activity
Journal Exercise

First, think about times when a close friend feels really bad about him or herself or is really struggling in some way. How would you respond to your friend in this situation (especially when you're at your best)? Please write down what you typically do, what you say, and note the tone in which you typically talk to your friends.

_____

_____

_____

_____

_____

_____

_____

_____

_____

_____

_____

_____

_____

_____

_____

Now think about times when you feel bad about yourself or are struggling. How do you typically respond to yourself in these situations? Please write down what you typically do, what you say, and note the tone in which you talk to yourself.

_____

_____

_____

_____

_____

_____

_____

_____

_____

_____

_____

_____

_____

_____

_____

_____

_____

_____

_____

_____

_____

_____

Did you notice a difference? If so, ask yourself why. What factors or fears come into play that lead you to treat yourself and others so differently?

_____
_____
_____
_____
_____
_____
_____
_____
_____
_____
_____
_____
_____
_____
_____
_____
_____
_____
_____
_____
_____
_____

Please write down how you think things might change if you responded to yourself in the same way you typically respond to a close friend when you're suffering.

_____

_____

_____

_____

_____

_____

_____

_____

_____

_____

_____

_____

_____

_____

_____

_____

_____

_____

_____

_____

_____

_____

_____

_____

_____

_____

_____

Chapter 8: Say Goodbye to Social Anxiety

Social anxiety cripples the lives of many people and can make it impossible for them to speak in public or even interact with others in large social settings. While some people experience it to this kind of devastating effect, many more find they have social anxiety to a lesser degree which can make them feel non-confident in the work place or among friends. It can then prevent them from fulfilling their potential in their careers or in their love lives.

Often social anxiety comes down to a feeling that they are somehow inadequate or that what they say isn't worth as much as what others say. People opt not to speak because they worry that what they say will be 'stupid'. At the same time they worry that they might stutter or stumble over their words and so not get their point across properly. That people will figure out that they're nervous and get bored waiting for them to t-t-t-t-talk…

One quick and easy way to improve the clarity of your speech as well as your vocabulary is to talk more slowly. The slower you talk the more time you'll have to think about the next thing you're about to say. It will also help you to project your voice more and you'll instantly sound clearer, deeper and more confident.

Use CBT and Become Socially Bulletproof

However, if you're in your own head and worrying about stuttering then you'll find this hard to do as you naturally speak more quickly when you're nervous. Ironically, it's worrying about getting a stutter that will give you a stutter. So how do you get out of your own head enough to slow down and speak more confidently?

As we discussed at the start of this book, in cognitive behavioral therapy, patients are told to use what is known as 'hypothesis testing'. Here you test the results of doing whatever it is you're anxious about in the hope that you find your concerns are unfounded. Interestingly though, it may actually be more useful if you find that you do say something stupid or stutter outrageously. The reason for that is that you'll this way test the worst-case scenario and learn in the process that there's nothing to be worried about. When teaching gymnasts to backflip on a crash mat, teachers get them to purposefully land badly on their neck or back in order to teach them that they will be okay and eliminate the fear (because again, it's being worried about backflipping that will make you pull out and hurt yourself mid-way).

One way you can test this is with strangers. Strike up conversation in a shop, bar or a coffee shop and don't worry at all about what you say or how you say it. In fact, try talking as strangely as possible about as dull a subject as possible. You'll never see them again so it doesn't matter and it's just an experiment. What you'll find though, is that they treat you just as anyone else. Politely and without drawing attention to your faults. That's human nature.

You see everyone is too busy worrying about how others see them to be able to judge everyone else. You see they are worried about how you'll react to what they say. If you needed any more proof that you're just as valuable and valid a human being as they are – there it is.

Activity

This worksheet includes 6 steps:
1. Clarifying the presenting problem(s)
2. Identifying the client's vulnerabilities by considering why the client more likely to experience this
problem(s) than another person
3. Identifying the client's triggers by considering the stimulus or source of the presenting problem(s)
4. Exploring coping strategies by considering the ways in which the client deals with the effects of
the presenting problem(s)
5. Listing the effects of current coping strategies, including how they make the client feel in the
short-term and long-term, along with the advantages and disadvantages of each strategy
6. Exploring alternative (more adaptive) coping strategies

Statement	Fact	Opinion
I'm dumb		
I'm unattractive		
I failed the exam		
I have no friends		
Nobody likes me		
I'm a selfish person		
This will be a disaster		
I will fail this test		
I'm not good enough		
I'm overweight		
I am single		
I will be single forever		
My family is disappointed in me		
I dislike my job		
I'm not good at my job		

Chapter 9: Changing Your Environment

The advice in this book can largely be split into two categories: the aspects that look at helping you to change your psychology – to appreciate things more, and to be kinder to yourself, and the aspects that tell you to look after yourself physically.

This option fits somewhere in that later category, though it is a little different again: changing the environment around you.

Looking after your skin, your hair, and your health will all help you to feel happier and better. You'll look healthier, and you'll have a glow that only comes with confidence and self-satisfaction.

But what about the environment around you? This is what gets overlooked so often, but people like Marie Kondo demonstrate how important this is to your overall happiness and satisfaction.

In fact, changing your environment can impact on your psychology in numerous ways and you can tap into any of these to be happier and healthier. Here are some things to consider.

Awe and Wonder

Here's one amazing example of how changing your environment can lead to a happier you: awe and wonder.

Imagine being primitive man and reaching the summit of a mountain. Imagine seeing valleys stretch out for miles in front of you, and you having never seen anything like it. This sheer scope and incredibly beauty would leave you basking in awe and wonder.

What's actually happening is that you are being forced to reconsider your place in the world – and that in turn is resulting in large amounts of literal rewiring in your brain. This process occurs alongside a cascade of hormones and neurotransmitters, which lead to the feeling of spiritual nourishment we are all familiar with.

When was the last time you saw something truly remarkable that changed your perspective? Whether it's looking through a telescope or going for a hike, try to find moments of awe. It could make your problems seem suddenly very small.

Tip: Going on a holiday or trip and changing your environment can also help you to overcome habits – as our environment contains triggers that make habits hard to kick.

The Healing Power of Nature

Another amazing way that the environment can change your feelings is by spending time in nature. This is where we evolved, and a lush natural environment once signaled an abundance of food and resources.

Thus, going for a walk in nature can have a similar effect on us now – triggering a reduced heart-rate and sense of calm. In fact, many great thinkers claim that going for "nature walks" was what helped them to come up with their best ideas.

Why? Because we are more creative when we are relaxed!

Your Home

Finally, don't underestimate the negative impact that a disorganized and untidy home can have on your mental state. If you can tidy and organize the space around you, then you can trigger huge changes in your mood, efficiency, and more.

Keeping things just a little more minimal is one of the best ways to do this, and that often means reducing clutter. This also means removing the things that you don't absolutely love – that don't bring you the most joy – which means the remainder will be only the things that create very positive emotions.

While you should cut down then, you should also improve quality. We've already discussed how investing in a better bathroom can help you to take better care of yourself. The same is true of your living room, where a plush couch can make a world of difference. And it's true of your bedroom, where a beautiful picture can make you feel wonderful.

Money doesn't buy happiness, but treating yourself to lasting items that surround you and make you feel amazing is one way to lift your spirits every single day!

Chapter 10: Why There's Really No Need for Low-Self Esteem

I know a lot of people who have almost non-existent self esteem, which I find both upsetting and difficult to understand. I've been practicing and sharing these self-care tips for years! Let me tell you, it's certainly better than wallowing in self-loathing. The thing is as well that these people have so much going for them that it defies all logic.

One of them is fancied by all our female friends, has got an amazing job working with celebrities and oozes charisma. A lot of people would swap their lives and bodies for his and yet he tells me all the time that he doesn't see himself as at all successful and doesn't 'like' himself.

I'm not among those people who would swap lives however as I'm perfectly happy with mine. That doesn't mean I don't admire features in him, but I realise that other people probably admire features in me. I, like them, have been given all the tools I need to be able to become whatever I want to be.

So rather than wishing I was more like someone, my time would be much better spent actually working towards becoming more like them in that area. I can pick the best assets of every person I admire and mimic them, and once you've learned those skills you'll appreciate them far more.

Want to be fitter? Get a gym membership.

Want to be more charismatic? Spend more time with other people and develop your posture and conversational style.

See these set-backs not as something to get upset about, but as challenges. Imagine you're in the film Rocky – a montage starts and you train until you're great at the things you want to be great at. I used to wish I could trade my life with celebrities who'd already found success and love – but the thrill is all in the chase.

You're a work in progress and if you work your way up to the top you can enjoy it properly with the sense of perspective that it required to get there. The minute you start working towards a goal like this you have purpose and a goal and you're not a 'nobody' anymore. You're a work in progress with grand dreams...

So there truly is no 'need' to be unhappy with yourself. If you're unhappy with an aspect of yourself, then change it. But the other reason I can't grasp the concept is that I wonder who these guys are measuring themselves against, or what counts as being 'successful' or 'worthwhile'.

The thing is, no one knows what the point of life is, so how can anyone tell you you're not doing it right? Someone who's earned no money might consider themselves a failure, but if they have lots of friends and family and have lead a full life then who can tell them that? So long as you pursue what you enjoy it doesn't matter if you're 'successful'.

Furthermore, no one should judge anyone else on their behaviour because they can't really know what's going on in that person's life. If you're acting unusual perhaps you have good motivation too? Perhaps there is method to your madness? Or perhaps you're experiencing trouble in your personal life. The real point is not to defer to the approval of others and not to let it control you. Only you can judge the value of what you do. Follow your own beliefs in your own way and you will be successful in your own eyes.

Conclusion Your Blueprint for Self-Care

That's the theory. Hopefully along the way you have learned a little about the importance of self-care and self-love, and perhaps what has led to low self-esteem and stress in the first place.

But now it's time to take that theory and turn it into something practical. From all we've learned, here is your blueprint to a happier and more fulfilled you:

Use mindfulness to better understand your self-talk

Place mantras around the home reminding yourself of your best qualities and to 'be kind' to yourself

Look after your appearance – spend time, money, and effort on your looks

Try loving kindness meditation

Look after your health by exercising regularly in a way that is light and sustainable

Dress well

Have a grooming regime and enjoy the process as much as the outcome!

Get 8 hours of GOOD sleep every night

Eat nutritious food, including

Spend time with people you love, practice the things you aren't confident in

Clear and tidy your home

Go on holidays, seek out moments of awe and wonder

Surround yourself with beautiful items that you love

Keep a journal and use it to write things that you are grateful for, and things you have done well/people have said about you that are flattering

Take all these steps every day, and you will be sure to enjoy feelings of self-love and contentment. Everything good will grow from there!

Self care for everyday life

30 easy ways you can start looking out for number one

Self-care is a big trend at the moment. But just because it is a trend, that doesn't mean it isn't also an extremely valuable activity, and one that we should ALL have been doing right from the start. Simply, self-care is looking after yourself. It means taking a moment to remind yourself you're doing okay, to enjoy yourself, to pamper yourself, and to eat well. These simple changes mean you attack life feeling and looking better, and they mean you actually get some enjoyment out of it along the way.

Seems simple, and yet it's something many people still don't do. So read on, and let's take a look at 30 easy ways you can start looking out for number one (that's you by the way.)

1.Meditate

Meditation means finding a quiet moment to direct your attention and focus on your state of mind. It is linked closely with mindfulness, and it can help you to find moments of calm where otherwise they didn't exist. Not only does this teach you to cope with life's biggest challenges, it also helps you to develop your grey matter!

2.Spend Time Outdoors

In beautiful lush environments, ideally! This triggers key hormonal changes, and helps to boost your health. It's also great for stimulating a sense of calm, not to mention creativity.

3.Keep a Photo by Your Bed

Keeping photos of friends to hand is a great way to remind yourself of the people you love. We evolved in small tribes, and studies show that seeing "faces" first thing in the morning can release key beneficial hormones.

4.Have the Right Grooming Regime

Grooming yourself is important if you want to look and feel your best. Moreover though, the simple act of taking care of yourself is an important ritual that can help you to find calm and release tension.

5.Exercise

Exercise improves your health and your looks, but also stimulates the release of beneficial neurotransmitters for an immediate mood boost.

6.Call Friends

Keeping photos around does wonders as we've seen, but better yet is to call a friend. This is especially important if you feel lonely from time to time. But either way, calling friends can help you to encourage a larger support network which is amazing for your psychological health. The same goes for family.

The best part? It helps them too, which is amazing for your own mood. Why not call on hands-free while cooking?

7.Message Friends

Messaging friends is an equally valuable way to stay in touch which can be just as healthy. Send a joke, or ask how a friend is doing, and it can open up a conversation that leaves you BOTH in much better moods.

8.Use Positive Mantras

Positive mantras are phrases that you can repeat to boost your mood or confidence. The great thing about this, is that it will not only offer a short term benefit, but in the long-term it can actually raise your general mood and esteem. That's because thinking this way can become habitual and internalized.

9.Make Note of Complements

It is often said that we give much greater importance to insults and things that go badly, than we do to complements and things that go well. To put a change to this, write down all the kind things you hear people say to you. Not only does this help you engage with those comments more, but it means that whenever you need to, you can read back through those comments!

10.List Things You're Grateful For

This is called 'cultivating gratitude' and it's something many of us could benefit from. Essentially, it means thinking about things that you're thankful for, and then taking the time to remind yourself of those things. This in turn allows you to focus on positive emotions and to remind yourself to enjoy what you already have – instead of always chasing after what is next.

11.Find Time for "You Time" Every Day

If you go through life constantly rushing from one job to the next, then you will never be able to actually enjoy your time. Not only that, but "you time" will allow you to pursue hobbies and interests that make you happy.

12.Get Enough Sleep

Getting sleep is crucial to your health, your mood, and even your long-term psychological well being. You owe it to yourself to get at least 8 hours.

13.Dress Yourself Well

Dressing well ensures you look better, which in turn means that others will perceive you differently. The "law of attraction" tells us that this can eventually lead to great things happening for us. Not only that, but when you dress yourself well, you send a sign to yourself and to others that you believe you are worth adorning in those nice clothes.

14.Decorate Your Home

Decorating your home well can mean surrounding yourself with things that make you happy. A tidy and well-presented home is also great for reducing stress that can come from clutter and disorganization. While you might not feel like you have the time, taking some time out of your schedule to clear your home and make it look beautiful can ensure that everything else you do feels and goes better.

15.Take Holiday

Just take the time off!

Too many people feel they have to work extremely hard all the time, and that they can never take a day off. If they do, then surely it will mean that they'll be slacking, and that they will look bad in the eyes of their employers. They'll be shirking responsibilities, leaving it to others, and doing a poor job!

You know what? If you take a day off today, no one is going to notice. And when you look back on your life years from now, you won't even remember. What you will remember is being ill from being overworked, or missing out on amazing opportunities.

16.Cut Out Toxic People

A toxic person is anyone who makes you feel bad about yourself regularly. While you can't easily cut someone out entirely if you will be encountering them in your daily life, what you can do is to create boundaries and avoid spending more time than necessary with them. You don't owe these people anything, and they won't change.

17. Learn to Say No

Many of us struggle to say no. This results in us taking on too much responsibility, and committing to too many different things. Learn to say no, and to spend time at home recuperating without a "reason." Life will get much easier and happier.

18. Enjoy Healthy Treats

Good food triggers a spike in happiness and reward hormones. If it's unhealthy, this enjoyment will be short lived and you'll soon feel stressed and anxious again. But if it's healthy, then the beneficial nutrients will help to improve your mood long term, not to mention fortifying your mind and body.

19 Take Sick Days

As before, it is important to recognize that there is no honor in refusing to ever take time off work. This goes double when it comes to sick days. Your health is more important than what your boss thinks of you, so if you're ill, do everyone a favour and call in sick!

20. See the Doctor

Likewise, when you're ill you should see a doctor. Think about what you would tell a family member. If they were limping and spluttering, you'd tell them to see a doctor. Show yourself the same respect and kindness!

21. Use Loving Kindness Meditation

Loving kindness meditation is a form of meditation where you focus on feelings of love and happiness that are directed toward yourself. You will be cultivating these emotions, so as to increase their abundance. It's a great practice that can help you feel warm and content throughout the day.

22. Pet a Dog or Cat

It's one of the best ways to trigger the release of feel good hormones. If you have the time and money to own a pet, then this is one of the best forms of therapy out there!

23. Keep Plants and Flowers in Your Home

Plants and flowers can help boost your mood and health in many ways. Looking at greenery can help you relax and stimulate creativity for instance, while the oxygen production may also be beneficial. Plus, caring for something is another great way to feel better about yourself.

24.Drink Plenty of Water

Drinking water is extremely important for your health. The more water you drink, the more you'll boost your energy level, mood, sleep, and more.

25.Enjoy "Bubble Time"

Bubble time is a term I coined. It essentially means enjoying tiny moments of complete peace and quiet and basking in the freedom you have during those moments.

For example, if you are taking an elevator somewhere, then you can take that time to simply relax. It's only a 1 or 2 minute journey, but in this 'bubble time' you don't need to worry about anything else!

26.Eat More Slowly

The more slowly you eat, the more you'll enjoy your food. This is also extremely good for your health, as eating quickly can lead to weight gain (we don't recognize when we're full), indigestion, and much more.

27.Make a Note of Things You're Looking Forward To

When you spend your life going from one crisis to another, or simply carrying out jobs, it can be hard to remember just how much exciting there is to look forward to.

These don't need to be big things like holidays (though that works too of course!). They can just as easily be tiny things: things like new movies that are coming out, the breakfast cereal you will have tomorrow, or finishing that book later on. Don't have things to look forward to? Get some!

28.Hit Snooze

There are so many self-help articles and books telling you how to wake up on time every time. There are countless entrepreneurs and self-help gurus claiming that you should get up at 4am every day.

And yet, when the alarm goes off early, you always just find yourself wanting to roll back over and go to sleep.

You know what? You've earned it! If it's the weekend, or if you have a bit of time spare, then hit snooze and enjoy those 10 extra minutes. They won't kill you! In fact, chances are that if you're that tired, then you actually need the time!

29.Learn the Difference Between Success and Happiness

This is a bigger one, but it's essential. Too many of us equate success to happiness, meaning that we think that 'doing well' is the same as 'living well'. It is not. And in fact, for many of us, success is a trap. When you start chasing success to the extent that you are no longer taking the time to enjoy your lifestyle, it means that you aren't going to benefit from any of that success.

Learn to enjoy each step along the way. And moreover, think about what the lifestyle you're chasing after will actually mean for your energy levels, your stress, and the time you get to spend with your family.

30. Use a Daylight Lamp

The last one is another easy one: get a daylight lamp! This is a light that mimics the rising of the sun, and creates a very similar wavelength. The value of such a lamp lies in its ability to affect your hormones and mental state similarly to the real sun. This can combat SAD (seasonal affective disorder) and drastically raise your mood.

So, there you have it! 30 easy things you can do to boost your mood, to fix your health, and to be happier and more content. But the most important takeaway is simply that you should be doing something to enhance your mood and well being. It's okay to need a bit of TLC from time to time, and it's okay to be the one to provide it!

Resource

Apps

Headspace www.headspace.com

The Headspace app is an app that serves as the perfect introduction to mindfulness meditation. It will guide you through the process of focussing your mind and calming your heartrate. It makes it very easy to learn, and you can then dip into the guided sessions whenever you need them. When you need a little downtime, or if you want to become generally calmer and happier, Headspace is a great option.

MindWave from NeuroSky
http://store.neurosky.com/

MindWave is an 'EEG' headset. This will allow you to measure your brainwaves, which can then be used in conjunction with an app in order to train you in order to be able to stay calmer and happier. Lots of exercises and games are included to help guide you through the process of taking better control over your mood and thoughts, and the results can be extremely powerful – potentially helping you improve you meditation skills in a fraction of the time.

Fabulous
https://www.thefabulous.co/

Fabulous is an app that is designed to help you set goals and stick to positive habits. It does this by using a number of different mantras and tips, and by using reminders. It has won awards for its design, and is one of the most pleasing apps on iOS or Android to look at and use!

That helps!

Books

Happy

Happy is a book from UK mentalist Derren Brown. While Derren usually puts his skills to work wowing audiences, in this book he instead focusses his understanding of psychology on another task: helping readers to be happier and more content. The general thrust focusses on the works of Seneca and other thinkers, who believe that learning to see the goodness in what you have – and even to accept that things sometimes go wrong – can be the most powerful way to improve your experience of the world and to be much happier as a result.

The Brain That Changes Itself

This book discusses the topic of neuroplasticity in great depth. For those not familiar, neuroplasticity is the science of the way the brain changes in response to learning and experiences. The simple fact is that your brain will grow and shrink in different regions in order to reflect the way you use it. If you use certain skills a lot, the brain areas that are responsible for those skills will get bigger and more developed… and vice versa!

This is important, because understanding this science essentially allows us to design the way our own brains work and to alter the way we think. This is one way that we can pick up bad thinking habits – or learn to eliminate them!

The Master Key System

In the book, we discussed the role of the "law of attraction." This discusses the way in which looking and acting a certain way can ultimately make us become a certain way. This book looks at how to tap into that power by knowing what you want and going after it. One of the biggest fans of this book is Terry Crews, and most of us would say he's a pretty happy and successful guy!

Other Tools and Resources

Shots of Awe
https://www.youtube.com/user/ShotsOfAwe
This is a YouTube channel that is all about awe cultivation. This is something that we discussed in the book – how seeing something or thinking something that changes your entire perspective on the world can bring about massive change in your brain and also fill you with positive and feel-good hormones.

Shots of awe helps to encourage this sensation by focusing in on truly amazing facts and then combining this with inspiration music and tightly edited imagery. It's a real experience, and each video lasts just a few minutes.

Tony Robbins: Finding Your Purpose
https://www.youtube.com/watch?v=qD8js_Ol2UE
Tony Robbins is one of the most well-known and respected coaches and authors on the subject of self-improvement and self-help. In this video he explains how to find your purpose in life. While this is a little more self- help than self-care, it's still a very important way to understand yourself better. When you know what it is you are trying to accomplish, you can become hugely more confident in yourself and you can gain a much better understanding of how to get where you want to be in quicker time.

Oprahmag.com
https://www.oprahmag.com/life/relationships-love/g25629970/positive- affirmations/

This is a list of positive mantras from none other than Opra. If you repeat these mantras daily, the aim is that it will help you to feel better about yourself. This works in the short term (and we recommend sticking these mantras onto little post-it notes) but it also works in the long term. That's because, over time, you will learn to make this kind of thinking habit.

Now, you will find yourself thinking positive things by default, rather than thinking negative things and "beating yourself up" all of the time!

Bullet Journal
https://www.amazon.com/Bullet-Journal-Hardcover-Notebook-Expandable/dp/B07L4GSGWD/ref=sr_1_1_sspa?keywords=bullet+journ al&qid=1572626175&sr=8-1-spons&psc=1&spLa=ZW5jcnlwdGVkUXVhbGlmaWVyPU EzSkdWQUI2V

1FKSDNQJmVuY3J5cHRlZElkPUEwNTAzNjEzQkxFODI wWldUWTNUJ
mVuY3J5cHRlZEFkSWQ9QTEwNDQ4NDUxM0dIODRL SEUxM1oxJndp
ZGdldE5hbWU9c3BfYXRmJmFjdGlvbj1jbGlja1JlZGl yZWN0JmRvTm90T G9nQ2xpY2s9dHJ1ZQ==

Throughout the book we talked at length about the power of journaling – about how you can benefit from writing down the things you are grateful for and the things that you like about yourself, or have done well. We also talked about the benefits of simply keeping a journal in order to keep a log of your life and to help you look back and appreciate everything that has happened/to better gain perspective and context for events. While this can be very powerful, you might be wondering how to structure all of this. One very popular option right now is to keep a bullet journal! This is a book designed to support bulleted lists and other information structured in a less conventional – but more artistic – manner.

Massage Chair

https://www.amazon.com/Tinycooper-Massage-Gravity-Lower-Back-Heating/dp/B07M8455YG/ref=sr_1_7?keywords=massage+chair&qid=1 572626194&sr=8-7

Self-care is about looking after your mindset yes, but it is also about indulging yourself and being kind to yourself. One great way to do that is with massage. And with a massage chair, you'll have endless massage on tap!

For one-on-one coaching please visit www.MLRuscsak.com

Melisa is all about authenticity, as anyone who's met her can attest. Whether you've seen her speak or talked with her at an event, or had a conversation with Melisa she is relaxed and candid. In the same way, her speaker bio doesn't just share the standard info about her credentials and speaking skills

"Motivational Keynote Speaker, Melisa Ruscsak works with individuals and organizations to amplify their communication, connection, and confidence so they can make an influential impact on the world. She mentors with passion, guiding her clients to effectively strengthen and elevate their leadership vision to new heights.

With over five years of corporate training experience, a knack for making meaningful connections with audiences, and an insatiable appetite for helping others maximize their potential, Melisa knows how to rock a platform, connect with a crowd and provide training so that others can effectively do the same.

Melisa's down-to-earth humor compels audiences to laugh while they learn. She engages groups from the moment she steps in front of them and leaves them with empowering tools and focused mindsets that they will use long after the lights have gone out on the event. Melisa is passionate about people, leadership, and successful businesses. She is especially inspired to help people take their careers - and themselves - to unprecedented levels.

When not speaking or training, Melisa can be found creating new worlds and stories within her literary world. Those works can either be found in stories for young adults or housed within screenplays.

www.ingramcontent.com/pod-product-compliance
Lightning Source LLC
Chambersburg PA
CBHW011223120626
46545CB00010B/3128